Robert Lundquist

After Mozart (Heroin On 5th Street)

set in Mrs Eaves
design and typesetting
by New River Press
edited by Robert Montgomery and Heathcote Ruthven,
with special thanks to Esme Lloyd and Jamie Lee

ISBN: 978-1-9996310-3-1

Thanks to the editors of The Nation, The Paris
Review, Poetry Now, Kayak, Quarry West, The
European Times, and Moving Parts Press.

For

Nazare Magaz

and

Lorca Bellamacina Montgomery

Dum in Spe

Robert Lindquist

AFTER MOZART (HEROIN ON 5TH STREET)

Oh our majesty who condemns us all
whose light shadows the promise of light
whose promise shadows the presence of light
whose presence is the absence of light
in whose absence the presence of light promised.

Oh our majesty who condemns us all
It is not the shadows that trace our lives
but a match of light
cupped between our hands in prayer
the spoons of which
measure both our hours and our days.

Oh our majesty who condemns us all
this is where the bare trees roam
their symphony their chorus
rising above the heroin tents
whose black tar beds
lay beneath a tattooed arm.

Oh our majesty who condemns us all
who clamps each vein upon each vein
whose fountain of blood
surrounding Fifth Street
hotels the language of our despair
and protects our throats of envy.

Oh our majesty who condemns us all
please see the shadows that present the light
please see the light that shadows the promise
forgotten by the childhood
lost in the moist smells of our addictions
lost in the thin scabs over our skin
our eyes see only the resin in our dreams
and our love is the dull ache in the crooks of our arms.

A PLACE FOR US TO SIT UNTIL MORNING

It is like drowning,
The water of the eyes spills back into the head
It coats the skull like honey
Until you can no longer hear the breathing.

And the breath?

The tongue patted the breath into buttons
To be sewn to the heart.

And the heart?

A fist soft even when clenched.

Was there a needle?

Yes, the needle slipped into the lungs
Where the breath first burned.

And the flame?

It is the tongue of the animal
Beginning to lap at the base of the spine.

What is the spine?

It is the loom.

And the thread?

The wet web in which we float.

Have we enough?

Yes, enough to knit the blood filled suit.

And the blood?

The rain clotted in the boards of this dark room.

And the room?

A place for us to sit until morning.

IT IS AT NIGHT

It is at night
when only the wings of birds
are heard inside their cages
the trains that run inside us
are filled with the blood of cattle
beneath the lamps of the trestle
a gull lies half eaten
and in the brush
a dog sleeps without hunger
it is at night
when the moths wake to what we have woven
and the one loud mouth
left in the street
is waiting
for his body
to make tomorrow's water
it is at night
when there is no place left to eat and drink
and we cannot waste a bit of tar or coal for our warmth
when the intersections are full of drunkness
and the fish hang like scarves beneath dark pools
when each leg shares our breath
and the bright boats
lowered to this water
are the tongues that held tonight's speech
now soft inside their lover
it is at night
when only the wings of birds
are heard inside their ages
and the trains that run inside us
are filled with the blood of cattle

POEM BEFORE VALENTINE'S DAY 2016

It is Sunday.

A day before Valentine's day.

The first quarter of a moon rising.

Right now, I am living in Downtown Los Angeles,
on the corner of 5th and Spring.
I am sitting on my couch, alone,
thinking about James Wright—
Thinking of his poem about horses—
The poem where he almost blossomed.

And I wonder what James Wright would write about if he
lived here—
Without lush—
Without nostrils breathing into the sweet face of hay—
Without the dark eyes of fur around him—
And again,
            without lush.

I think he would write about the tents three blocks from
here
                                              and
the calvary therein,
                  fast asleep.
I think he would write about that one part
                                    absent of light
freezing the right for everyone
                        to share the same stream.

I think how
his trembling hands
would part the bloody trash

between the tents.
How he would
bless each bottle of relief
with his own
trembling
hands.
      And last,
how he would wait for his own breath to still,
waiting for his own breath to still—
The sky seemingly still—
For a moment—
Only.

A POEM A REFLECTION

It is 3:30 in the afternoon
The windows of the apartments
above The Onyx Lounge
reflect green leaves
Reflect blossoms
cracked lamp posts
dull birds
break lights
All
that is
the time
of this day
reflected
Reflected
around
two hands
two lonely hands
cupped
around
a
glass
A reflection
in the windows
of the apartments
above
the Onyx Lounge
Hands around a glass
A reflection
A moment
All
that is the time
of this day
reflected
Two hands
around
a glass

in a room
In a room
of
The Alexandria Hotel
A reflection
of a hotel
of a hotel
A reflection
of a hotel
in the windows
above
The Onyx Lounge
The Onyx Lounge
a reflection
in the windows
of The Rowan Building
A reflection
All
that is the time
of this day
3:30 in the afternoon
cracked lampposts
dull birds
break lights
green leaves
with blossoms
blossoms
reflected on this day
On this day
forever
Forever
in your lonely hands
in your lonely hands
of cupped warmth
Where
in the windows
Where in the windows
are you?

DORIAN

She used to work at Denny's. She drove a Honda Civic.
Sometimes, she held hands with Devin in a soft light.
Before she became homeless, she wanted a child. Devin
said, we cannot afford a child. She wanted a child to keep
Devin from leaving. Devin left just before Thanksgiving.
Her name was Dorian. One night, Dorian called her one
relative, her sister. Her sister did not answer. Dorian sat
on a stool in her kitchen. The sun rose twice. Dorian
called Devin. Devin did not answer. The sun rose once
more. Dorian slept.

The skin of her eyes pull down the life
missing in one eye. From words
unspoken, when her lips part, her teeth
bite down on the knuckle of her loss
When her lips part the names who
sorrow her tear at the cuticle
of each finger, each finger bleeding
on the names of her sorrow.
From words
unspoken water spreads across her cheeks
onto the lips of each face now missing .
The crease in her throat folds back on the one
sad feeling left
behind. The one sad feeling
tilts her head as if to see tomorrow and
tomorrow always comes.

Dorian wanted to feel her baby asleep on her chest. She
wanted to feel her baby's breath on her cheek. She wanted
to see each eye open at the same time. She wanted to teach
her baby to kiss. She wanted a child to keep Devin from
leaving. She told her sister, I think Devin is going to leave
me. She pressed Devin to make love more often. When

Devin left, she called her sister. Her sister did not answer. She found Devin's bottle of Jack Daniel's. She did not understand why Devin drank. She poured herself a Jack Daniel's with Coke. She began to forget about Devin. She poured herself another Jack Daniel's with Coke. She sat on a stool in the kitchen. She called her sister a second time. Again her sister did not answer. She sat on a stool in the kitchen. The sun rose three times. She sat on a stool looking into an empty glass. The ice had melted. The glass had dried.

BREACH

There was no easy solution.
Those who would have our death ate well all morning.
Something moved into the brush
and a car followed.

What should we have done?
All day the shadows stayed close to the buildings,
Clouds that held this heat to earth crept into cold water.
Two boys walking along the tracks
Waited to enter the tunnel to hold hands.

So far no conclusion.
Is it true we were born to a damaged people;
or that night arrives one lamp less to each room?
She rode that bus through the dark
And became ill waking next to a man she had never met.

IF I GO TO THE RIVER

No wind this morning.
If I go to the river ducks will be towing
Their young.
Eucalyptus leaves bobbing in their wake.
To get there I will follow the tracks
Through a ravine of cattail
To a trestle.
A small path descends
To the mouth of the river
Opening seaward.
A young girl with a broken shovel
Is digging for clams,
speckled gulls folding wings beside her.

ON A DARKENING ROAD

This evening the tide is low.
Ducks walk through bunched beds of kelp
Looking for insects.
In the mountains they are clearing the orchards;
Apples rumble into boxes,
A fine mist collects between the branches.
On a darkening road
A man takes a corner too fast.
He stumbles to his trunk to put out a flare.
Another car cannot see him.
It is dusk.
The sky is in blossom.
Small birds fly east.

THE BLOOD MYTH

The blood of a woman and the blood of a horse
Are running through the field.

There is the odor of birth
There are the arrows of gull's feet to direct them

The blood of the woman teaches the blood of the horse
her name

The woman reaches inside the horse
to find the body of a bird without shadow

The horse who is black finds fresh mind breathing beneath
stone

The woman kneeling
Steals eggs of a pheasant whose flight is trapped inside her

The gull's wing broken flies without sound

NOW THE BLOSSOMS FIRST THE CROWS

Blossoms
and crows,
a few bits of unripe fruit,
inside the orchard.
Now the blossoms,
first the crows;
the white boat burning
in a ditch
once used for water.
After blossoms
the small green fruit
and the pure milk
poured into the field for profit.
An illness:
now the strange writings of pharmacies,
a rifle opening
inside the orchard,
then blossoms.
Enough proposals written for feed.
Now
the small green fruit.
And before,
before the branch the wing or the flower,
I have loved you,
all my life
the branch and the bud that has no closing.
Now the blossoms,
first the crows.
A rifle opens.
After blossoms the small green fruit
and the pure milk poured into the field
for profit,
then blossoms.
An illness:

there is something
a kind suffering of,
between the fields of the first crow,
the pure milk,
and the white boat burning.
I have loved you,
all my life.
The small green fruit,
blossoms,
my rifle,
I have loved you,
the branch and the bud,
crows,
that has no closing
between each season;
now
the blossoms,
first the crows.

WITH BOTH HANDS

It is evening.
The cliffs behind her
slide into the bay.
Along the foam of each wave
I watch one hand sweeping lady bugs onto the sand.
Below the orange light,
her numbers fall steadily inside her lungs.
He watches her—
The hem of her blue dress,
her wet bare feet.
If she turns around,
her yellow eyes might see him
drown in her own black water.
He is trying to understand her decision.
For a moment,
he shares her decision;
he thinks about going with her.
Five miles from here,
in the white light of chemotherapy,
numbers rise and fall
between the walls of each room.
Each night the janitor buffs out
the heel marks beneath each chair.
Back on the sand,
she stays with her back to him,
gently lifting each tiny wing.
Again, he thinks of going with her.
Without children, without family,
he imagines the lesions of loneliness;
Will she turn around and walk to him?
He is thinking about the morphine left over.
She is kneeling now.
She is lifting each body.
She is using both hands.

POEM OF THE FLIGHT

I am not able to watch the sun rise
From the rafters of the church.

I do not have wings to lift doors of darkness.

I have no tail to flirt with the logic of water,

It is not easy to give up the flesh,
I am afraid if I do,
The corpse that I find
Will not be my own.

It is not easy for me to be a man now,
To watch other men bait hooks
Letting them float on the surface
Waiting for the gulls to dive,

The bait swallowed,
The white necks turn red in flight;
The screams are reeled in like fish.

It is not easy for me to watch this.

The flesh still hangs
Like the coat I never wear
In the closet.

The moon sets
And the boats row off without me.

YOU DOCUMENT EVERYTHING

beginning with the rain.
Next, the sun shining over the boats
bobbing up and down in calm waters,
and you, rising above the distance
between sun and shade,
disappearing, turning into cloud,
the drops of water falling off you
between the flowers and the leaves,
and the drops of dew around you.
Then, in the damp ridge of oak trees,
you hover over a single red mushroom,
recording the sounds of spores
opening around fallen leaves.
To chronicle is to chronicle loss.
Like the tide
carrying away the people we love
tracing the people we love.
We trace.
We rain.
We disappear into clouds.
The drops of water fall off us.

TWO LEAVES PRESSED AGAINST SPEECH

Two leaves
pressed against speech
you come
absent of tongue to me
through the fields of lettuce
and the orchards
where the moths have lain their wings;
against the blossoms
you come
through the ripening of figs
into the cloths
dipped in milk
to wrap
the frost bent limbs
of young trees
you come
absent of tongue to me
as I am pouring
thin glasses of steam
for your sleep;
there are long trains of sand
crossing the sea
and you are coming
with the first boats rising
their sails
white blue and red;
at dawn
the full wake of your mouth
searching
for the light of fish
in darkness
you come
two leaves pressed against speech;
in the burnt grass where brush-colored birds
feed on the cracked seeds
of your passing.

INSIDE THE WOMB

Inside the womb blood drips onto slate
The blood forks the earth it speaks in both tongues

Inside a crib of antlers guards the breath
Of a child wrapped in moonlight and tobacco

Inside small boys are belayed through a cornice in the heart
Where candles still burn for the births
Who have lain like mud between thighs

Inside the mother and father discuss an eclipse
The speak of ghosts whose dreams are slow turnings in the
belly

They remember the last one
A boy whose flesh sputtered like a wet fuse

And now you my sister your spine disintegrating inch by inch
Until the final push there will drop a sack
Crumpled by the mortar raining inside you

But I am not far
In this cave I am as safe as the larvae of insects
Tucked under stone

I await the other members of our expedition

When they come they will bring lungs of iron
And the buttery lights of incubation
They will bring the last of our ropes slings and Carabiner

When we descend through those hips of quartz
I promise you all things will be a solid ringing
Even our hatchets and chisels will sweat

YOU WANT

the trees to speak to the wind,
cool off the streets downtown,
the sweat off the strollers
halfway down Spring Street,
born on Main Street,
the sweat born on Los Angeles street,
rings of sweat,
bracelets of sweat,
hands
raking hrough the trash on Hill street,
sifting through the trash on Olive street,
their sweat
pouring on the grease-coated empty coke bottle
on Figueroa street;
the sweat of cooks,
maids.
jewelers.
The sweat of the dress makers.
The sweat of the three string guitar players sweating for
quarters on Broadway.
The sweat of baristas just arrived from Maryland
The sweat of bus drivers from South Central
The sweat of cops
the same sweat
as crooks generation after generation
                                        after generation
down the gutters of Angels Flight
into the last vegetable stall
in Central Market.
Somewhere now a lost dog is wailing.
Somewhere now a lost baby is crying.
Somewhere after another drink is poured;
somewhere on 5th Street
after another arm, another toe,
the back of a wrist is punctured.
Somewhere after your last lie,
Somewhere before your last kiss when you felt what you
hoped to feel forever.

BIRD

As I walk towards the porch of the clinic,
my shoes break dry grass.
Niao sits on the porch,
burrowing her face into her mother's chest.
As I come closer,
Niao begins to kick and scratch.
I remember the day Niao lost her language
how the wind over the steps of the orphanage
chafed Niao's face, rocked her silence, rocked her cradle.
I remember my own silence
visiting my mother in Barlow's Sanitarium,
the softest part of me, like the softest part of Niao,
frightened of thumbs I could not see.
Before I reach the porch,
Niao wraps her arms tightly around her mother,
hollow bones trembling.
I say hello—
Niao clenches her fists.
I sit down on the porch and her mother asks,
what is wrong with her?
Her eyes stare through me.
I say,
Niao lives in the space between your tears,
in the first time held in your arms;
you are still her arms around her.
I say,
the language of her dreams still calls to her in her sleep.
I say,
you are like a cricket, outside her bedroom window,
startled by the sounds rising in the heat between her wings.

TO THE POET WILLIAM EVERSON

Bill, we smoke the same cigars, hard leaves wrapped
By the Italians in Pennsylvania.
And second to Hennessy, I have a passion for Jack
Daniel's.
In moonlight I have spread my fingers across the stone
walls
Of Robinson Jeffers' fort.
And again, last night, while weeping in the sand of a
friend's death
I heard the full bellies of seals slapping
Against a cold wave.
I have watched this tide night end and night out
Entering the same beach.
I have listened to the wings folding
Between the dark rocks above me.
And still,
This,
This thick muscle fastened to the roof of warning,
This tongue
Sheathed in the crack of a shark's eye,
Is silent.
Bill, of what use are lips that not accept the tongue's heat;
Flesh that warps from fear of the dream.
Why do I fear these winged rats sleeping inside me,
Or their yellow eyes widening for the flight.
The heart's blood freezes to the stump,
The body sap clotted.
I am sure death's itch is the nettle's rash beneath my wrists
As the crushed bone rots.
And as the bone rots
The muscles flatten into whips,
The blood tongue is muted.
With the tongue silent the lip's flesh cracks,
The knotted pulse breathes through my fists.

TRYING TO REMEMBER

a hill
where sky ends
and clouds bend
the tops of the trees—
Trying to remember sky
lost to the sea,
ending in a thin whist
each card dealt
to remember,
as dogs remember,
as the Clark's Nutcracker
remembers:
perfectly—
How we amble now
with a small bag
filled with each suit
to deal one more day—
Like the sky
and, now, like the sea,
hoping, ourselves,
like the sky,
like the sea
to be remembered,
we wrap ourselves around a ridge
above a sky above a sea
to the tops of trees
covered with leaves
we. Ourselves, covered with leaves,
trying to remember
a hill
where sky ends
where the clouds bend
trying to remember
before tomorrow

when you ask
about the sea
lost to a game,
where,
the cards dealt
perfectly
wrapped a hill
with dogs
with birds with sky
ending
as the clouds
at the tops of the trees.

TODAY THERE IS AN END TO THE SKY

there, at the end of these trees.
This is normal.
But tomorrow, the sky will end
where we have lost the sea
inside a hole in the ice—
And the day after
the sky will end
in the small bag
with deep pockets
you carry overnight
whenever you want to sleep
hoping to be forgotten—

No one will know what to do
once the sky ends.
For protection,
wrap yourself around a hill
(that you cannot see)
so there is, at least,
a place for your skin—
So that, once the sky ends
you can reach into your bag,
slip your hand inside a pocket,
pull out a piece of you you remember,
roll over, look up, and see the stars for ever.

JOURNEY

Her eyes never close. Still she sleeps and dreams
of the pale young man who rides alone. On a train he
rides, black drapes surround him.

I entered the water at dusk. A single star shining
above me. From a green depth I was able to see what
had always preceded me: each of us entering the other,
the soft pads of our feet slowly turning the earth.
Because I had given up breath I was able to hear what
had not yet reached the others. I understood distance.
I saw trains passing over me in the night.

Her eyes never close. Still she sleeps and dreams
of the pale young man holding a mirror. It is always
her face and not his. If he touches his mouth, it is her
lips that close like a warm animal around the tips
of his fingers. If he breathes onto the glass, it is
odor that he smells. At times their eyes meet
but they never speak. There is something travelling
inside them.

At dusk I entered theater without her, a single
star shining above me. From this green depth I saw
what had always preceded me. Each of us entered
ourselves. From a distance I heard what had not yet
reached the others: the hum of the earth driving our
feet to their destinations, the rustle of curtains
her pale hands drew through the room in which I had
always travelled, and the sound of the trains she would
ride passing over me in the night.

THE ROOM

In a boy's room a penis is caressed. The red veins
stretch into the moist palm. He is dreaming of a
woman whose lips are as full as his thumb. He is
frightened of the wet leaves she has wrapped around him.

In the room next door a girl has touched he warmth
inside her. With her fingers she strokes the dark throat of
her sex.
She is dreaming of no man in particular. She touches the
skin
he has kissed on her neck.

Night enters the boy's room, but is not noticed.
The darkness crawls like a worm into the folds of his flesh.
Waiting for the wings to erupt inside him, the dew he has
dressed
walks from his sleep.

A light breaks into the girl's room. Through the
curtains
it gives the shadows that will fold like hands upon her face.
It has stoles the birds that would sing at her window. the
tide
that would feed her each morning no longer waits on the
shore
where she wakes.

COLD WATER

It was December in London. I had on a thin coat. I was with
Nick. We called a taxi, for a ride home, for warmth. When
we arrived, I remember you asking Nick, How's it going? If
I could have replied, I would have told you: It is almost like
sleep. It is almost like dreaming. It is like letters tucked away
unread. It is like music in slow motion. It is like silk flowers.
It is soft to the touch. It is bright, yet it freezes your heart.
You remember him. You remember why you stopped reading
his letters. Not because of the heat these letters raised inside
you; the opposite, they lifted you into a bed as cold as the
room you entered in London, in December. You were with
Nick. I had been drinking. I was sleeping. I was dreaming
of smoke. I was dreaming of water. I was dreaming of silk
flowers.
In the street below, someone is moving out of an apartment
in the middle of the night. Someone is yelling. Someone
is standing in the doorway, holding a bottle of scotch. The
neighbors find him repulsive. They hear him at night, angry,
yelling obscenities. They all have the telephone number of
his friend Nick; to call Nick in case of emergencies. There
have been several. Like the night he remembered burning
his hand on the exhaust pipe of his parents car while chasing
them. He remembers his mother touching his hand. Her
hand limp, as if she were dead. She smelled of scotch. It was
just after noon. The night before, she arrived home in a taxi
after midnight. She was wearing a summer dress. She was
holding silk flowers.
In slow motion, he watches his hand pick up a bottle of
rubbing alcohol and place it to his lips. Before this, before
placing the bottle to his lips, the neighbors could hear him
again screaming and called Nick, then called the police.
When the police arrived he was completely sober. Then
he lost consciousness, When he woke up in the hospital he
smelled flowers. He smelled smoke. He smelled sweat. His
own water was not warm, it felt cold, ice cold. Cold through
his hair. Cold through his fingernails. Cold through his
heart.

TITA'S PAIN

Tita's pain is a sky without wings;
birds inside too small to remember.
Tita's pain dissolves the butterflies and the window panes.
Therefore,
Tita's pain is a sky without wings,
birds inside too small to remember,
inside a morning too lonely to imagine:
a morning full of a prayer to be touched,
a morning full of tears of blood,
a morning without imagination,
a morning
where all of the animals that share her skin
scratch the light in her eyes—
the blood beneath slowly spreading—
Tita quietly swollen in her pain.

When Tita was a child,
Tita's mother, Mercedes,
named her asquerosa
named her detestable—
Tita's mother, Mercedes,
named her el dolor,
named her,
sky without wings,
named her all of the birds too small to remember—
Tita
too small to remember,
Tita, all night
against the butterflies
dissolved against the window panes,
Tita,
inside a morning too lonely to imagine,
inside a morning full of a prayer to be touched,
a morning full of tears and blood,

a morning without imagination,
a morning
where all of the animals that share her skin
scratch the light in her eyes, and
scratch the night around her mother—
until Tita,
asquerosa,
detestable,
el dolor,
swollen,
bruised,
quietly
Tita.

Before Tita's father, Antonio, left home forever,
and after his book on Fernando Zobel,
and before the butterflies and the windowpanes,
before the birds
too small to remember,
Tita,
before her father, Antonio,
swollen,
too lost to remember,
Antonio named her curiosidad,
named her sorpresa—
Then he walked, naked,
into the Prado,
naked through the glass,
the shard's of Tita's hope
to be touched
scattered inside a morning
too lonely to imagine—
a morning full of tears of blood,
a morning too full of imagination,
a morning
where all of the animals that share her skin
scratch the light in her father's eyes,

scratch the face of the syringe
above the paintings by her Godfather Fernando--
Her father,
Antonio,
once curious,
once surprised,
once
curious,
and
surprised—
Tita's father's pain
swollen,
bruised,
quietly
inside
Tita.

Tita had a brother, Juan, whom she adored—
For example,
when he went to the dentist,
Tita ate rocks to go with him—
However
her brother
scattered inside a morning
too dark to remember, and, before
his father swollen,
before his father still as a moth against the glass,
his father still as a sky without wings,
and,
before his own hands started to shake,
and,
before he could not eat, and, before Tita
waiting, desperate, for his touch,
Tita had a brother she adored—
Tita had a brother she adored,
the shards of her hope
too sharp—

too sharp
for her brother's morning of tears—
too sharp
for the mourning of his imagination—
a morning,
a mourning,
where all of the animals that share his skin
scratch the light in his eyes—
the blood beneath,
the blood beneath his eyes swollen,
bruised—
quietly
Mercedes,
quietly
Antonio,
quietly
Juan,
quietly
Tita
quietly
swollen
in pain.

AFTER THE RAFTERS

It was one in the afternoon that I slammed on my breaks.
On the Pacific coast highway, in Santa Monica, six pelicans
suddenly holding themselves completely still above my
car--Not westward, diving from above the shore, the waves
over tiny crabs sweeping back into the sea. Not westward.
Above my car. Six pelicans holding themselves completely
still. Over me.
Even though we also do this, suspend ourselves for
however long it takes, seeing the pelicans was like seeing an
arm that stops at the elbow. In reality, I could see a hand
clenching air, the metal of the crash wobbling inside a
wrist lying in the street.
The day before, the day after a storm, I picked a bird
out of the palm fronds in my front yard. I could feel the
storm, limp now, inside my hands: the legs of the storm,
fallen from the trees, receding, walking away as I held the
dead bird; the legs of the storm crushing tiny bones inside
scattered nests.
My father always kept his garage pristine. It was a museum
of old tobacco cans, old coffee cans, cans that held the
bandaids he placed over my scraped knees. Each can of
screws, bolts, nails, string nested beneath the wings of the
open rafters. Suspended from the rafters over one corner
of the garage was a bag he build wood stairs beneath so
I could begin a ritual that bound us together our entire
lives: One two three one two three, my hands taped to my
wrists-- one two three one two three, faster now, faster
now, end with a hook to hook the jaw I saw beneath the
rafters built by a man whose wings seemed to spread.
A Christian myth portrays Christ as a mother pelican
slicing her breast open with her bill to save her young
from starvation. In the world to which I am more familiar,
pelicans suspend themselves over me for reasons I do
not understand. What I do know, is that to wait is to

understand what is difficult to comprehend. Like the endless relationship between tides, crabs, and the moon. Like the relationship between nests and the legs of storms. Like the relationship between a young boy and his father, both of whom, taught to hit a bag faster and faster as if their arms would last as long as it takes.

AN APOLOGY

Breathing now an imposition?
Conversation, violence?

You of my forever sorrow who breathes lastly—
Now knowing between us the events to come—
Events I could not imagine,
and what I could not imagine you could not forgive,
could not forgive what I could not mind
                                        Between us
The events to come—
To come lastly.

To come lastly,
A place placed after all others;
A place placed after
                        The events to come.

Events I did not understand—
Obscured by the events early in my own life—
As if a chest, open, yet never with toys
closed the play, in my own mind, to understand
                                        The pain
Draped over me,
and now the pain draped over you.

A pain so obscure
I did not understand the moment
                            Before the moment
you knew you were dying—
                        That moment—
The moment before the moment—
You seemed to expect me to know and understand,
and, perhaps, I should have

*

The porch on which we sat
sailing our poems into the fog
stood at the end of a dirt road.
In the distance stood the sea.
The wounds of seals festering as they cried
long into the beds of kelp each night.

As you later said,
We only embarrassed ourselves—
Our desire to shine in the literary world
capsized any social grace--
The irony—
Understanding the mind of the other
blinded by our convictions of the other.

To come lastly—
A place placed after all others—
A place placed after
                    the events to come.

It will be like trying to understand
the next thought or feeling before the next thought or
feeling
It will be like closing your eyes before your eyes close
It will be like music through an open window
It will be speaking your last thought--

It will be
like the porch with the chairs
                        on which
neither of us is now sitting.
The porch of my thought,
you will be dying without me—
The image of us now,

strolling the deck of a ship slowly sinking—

But for now,
the leaves twirl on the end of their branch,
like the toys of children,
spinning through the wind—
Each of us,
falling through the wind, lastly—
A place placed after all others—
A place placed after the events to come.

PART TWO

a hope
of a thinking man's
coming
word
in the heart,

Paul Celan, from Todnauberg

THE SOMETHING MORE. A SIMPLE EXPLANATION

The Waiting,
   The Waiting For The Something More

         From
Heidegger

assembled

        through Years
of letters to and from.

Assembled
   after
     a reading
      in Frankfurt,
       Celan
        reading
"Todnauberg",

and

after

talking inside the Thinking Hut
      and
        walking through
a meadow

  and

standing in a clearing in the forest,
      Celan waited

For The Something More

from Heidegger.

*

Can you imagine waiting for The Something More from
Heidegger?

A simple speech—
          speech unbroken
                    for Worlds
                              broken—

Flowers
          about the thinking hut
                    bloomed—
The eight point star of David?
                    Or simply
                              flowers for the table.

Can you imagine Celan waiting for The Something More
from Heidegger?

Waiting
          with all his heart
                    for a heart speaking from the heart—

Speaking
as a clearing in the forest speaks
                              of light
                              after the trees have
fallen—

                              After the trees

fallen—

Light broken

clears the forest

of light broken.

*

And what about the language needing to be invented to
discuss The Something More?

For Heidegger
                language resided in a clearing in the forest;
                                        always
meaning something more

            but

never
            meaning something less
                    than
                            a clearing in the forest, for
Celan—

For
        Celan
                the clearing in the forest
                                finally meant
a knife
            meant for the heart
                      but the heart
                              meant for
poems

meant a heart

                    silenced
                              by a river.

                              *

The question for Celan?

how much
water
runs through Paris
each day?
Enough
to stop
one breath
at a time
And this time
by a river
inside Paris,
enough
to stop
this heart
this time
stop
this
breath
this
time.

                              *

Once,
          I waited

                    for my own
Something More—
                    it had to do with Love—
                              it had to do with being loved—
But
          it never had to do
                    with my love
                              for a Nation.
It never had to do
                    with the Eternal Waiting—
                              For a kind of
validation

in whose absence

          I no longer

                    exist.

In this regard,
                    To Exist—
                    I wonder,
after his reading of Todnauberg—
                    and
                              after talking
                                        inside
                                        the
thinking hut- -
And after
          a walk
                    through a meadow,
                              and after
                              standing in a clearing in the
forest,
and after suggesting to Heidegger,

The Something More—

                    Was
                        Celan thinking,
                                silence by a
river?
Enough water
                to stop one breath
                                at a time?
While living
            in a world
                    constructed by his mind,
or,
        living in a world
                    constructing his mind?

That is,
        is there pain
                turning the world
                            inside out—
                                    or worlds
                                        simply
                                            turning

inside
pain.

How awful
In
The End

Celan
tethered
to Heidegger

Light

minded

On
Light.

        *

After Celan walked into the Seine,
                        Heidegger
expressed sadness,

admiration for Celan's poetry.
But
    did Heidegger
        admire
           Celan?
Did Heidegger
        ever
          really
             understand
                  Celan's waiting
for
The Something More? A
          Simple explanation?

Did he understand
        Celan,
          once a child,
             grasped the sun
and the moon of his parent's eyes. That,
    without
        The Something More,

Celan lost his grasp
        for the moon,

lost his grasp
                for the sun—
                        A shadow of
                                himself
walking, forever, into the Seine—

Did Heidegger
                ever
                        really understand
                                Why?
                                        years of
letters

back and forth

                back and forth
did he?
        Heidegger—
                The great thinker,
                        In the absence
                                from himself,

for himself,

of

        The Something More
cease to exist?

                like
the water
        running through Paris,
                it's shadows
                        now
                                beneath
                                        a side of
light

somewhere

    lighting

    each side

    of light,

    perhaps to light

    a new page?

Perhaps—
    Perhaps,
        only Celan
            encouraged Heidegger
                    to,
                    finally,
                    himself, Exist
                      by

stating,

The Something More.

A STREET

A child is sitting
in the shade of an elm tree,

                                   tapping the trunk five
times for luck.
He is watching his hand carefully.

                               A small Beagle pup lies
beside him,

drips of sweat bead its tongue.
Suddenly the child stops

                    holds his breath

                         grits his teeth,

one tear forming in his eyes.
Finally,
        he surrenders
                  taps the tree once more,
                          five.
In the shade of an elm tree
                  a child surrenders to a voice
inside him:

                              even
numbers taste like sugar

                              even
numbers are soft like breasts.
A fist beats inside the child's head,
                  the fist beats five times,

the child subtracts one:
                       Father, why do
you carry a gun to work each night?

The child is running
        up the steps of his porch,
                carrying a glass jar in

both hands.
In the jar are the sweet translucent stems of grass
                                 picked to chew
before sleep each night;
When he falls his hands begin to pray
                             his face follows this
prayer:
                                 an odd number
is the color of blood
                                 an odd number
breaks like glass against your chin.

The boy's mother is lying in bed,
                his father,
                        putting on his rags to
go inside doorways

hiding inside doorways;
the gun for the holster lying on the bed,
                        lying on the bed,
                            a fist beating
inside his mother, inside his father

slamming its knuckles against their hearts,
one, two, three, four, five six, steps to the door.
                               an odd number
is the color of blood,
                               an odd number
breaks like glass....

The bandages around the boy's chin are white and clean:
                          even numbers taste like
sugar,
                          even numbers are soft
like breasts.

*

The room is dark where my mother lies sleeping.
                                                    The
breath between her lips

breaks like glass inside her room.
I walk over to her face;
                    the water from her eyes spills across her
cheeks.

one,

two,

three,

four,

five times before she wakes.
Before she speaks,
                    I subtract one number from the
room in which she lies.
                                        Even numbers
make a cold room warm.
                                        Even numbers
dry your eyes and never die.

Her words chip inside me like the numbers five or fifteen,
                                        her words tear the
lining from the even numbers of hope.
I am eleven years old today.
                    I have walked through the last
year of my life
dreaming of the blue bicycle parked in the living room.
Ten gears to ride with.
                    Two sprockets each.
                                        As I shift two at
a time

until I reach the number

ten

Lying in the mustard grass at the end of the street

my blue

bicycle lies beside me;
black beetles pop from between the weeds;

stink the air.

Today your mother weeps and sleeps.
Today you are given a blue bicycle and you hide in the
weeds.

*

When I sit it to eat

there is someone I have recently

only seen in

darkness.
For weeks she has taken her food inside her room.

Now

she eats

beside me;
pale as her napkin in front of her,

thin as the fork she takes to

eat.
With lips taut as the meat on her plate,

she speaks to me,
" I am leaving...

There is somewhere I

have to go...

I am sick and you

cannot breathe the air in which

I

live."

The man beside her chews his food and weeps,
The man who carries a gun to work is weeping.

I cut my meat into five pieces and listen

I cut my meat into five

pieces

                                        Subtract the
cube I put between my lips.
It is alright to breathe on even numbers
It is all right to chew the odd piece down.

"I am leaving...there is somewhere I have to go...
I am sick and you cannot breathe the air in which I live."

The man beside her chews his food and weeps.
                                        The man who
carries a gun to work is weeping.

He is dressed in the rags he wears to work each night;
                                        the tears spin
across his lips

into two even rows...
It is alright to breathe on even numbers.

When he speaks it is not to us
                            but to the palms of his hands,
When he speaks
            it is to someone I have never heard him
mention,

It is alright to chew the odd one down.

                        *

When I leave the kitchen table
                        I am trying to understand the
word "tuberculosis".
I am sitting on the back porch,
                        the light spilling into the
black grass.

60

Slowly
the spectators inside me begin to applaud.
                                        Slowly
the voices inside me
                grow louder than the voices outside me,
                                                louder
than the voices inside me:

Each of us is responsible for the other.

Through the darkness a man seems to walk towards me,
                                hands cupped in
prayer.
We are not special.

A child seems to show his face from the shadows
                                and sits beside me.
We can spare none of us.

The man takes his hands from his face.

We need you.

The man takes his hands from his face
                                and peels the skin
from my eyes.

Each of us is responsible for the other.

The man twists his tongue in the air
                        to crack the buds of phlegm
rising.

We are not special.

In the man's hands the lids of my eyes
                                flap like beetles freshly
turned.

We can spare none of us.

The lips of the child part to plugs of moist ash.

We need you,

And the man's hands breathe to bleed
                                    back and forth back
and forth.

We are not special.

And the child's mouth closes upon my mouth,

Back and forth.

Each of us responsible for the other.

                              *

I am standing in the hallway
                    in the middle of the night.
                                        I am
waiting.
                                                  I
am waiting for the house
to shake itself free from the earth;
                    to shake itself free
                              from my flesh.
I am running
        where my legs stand still
                    in the middle of the night.
                                                  I
am trying to remember
            why
                    I get up to stand here

whenever I dream of her;

why
     I shake
          until I am able to see
               the walls,
                    and why I seem
to be standing still
                   where the rug
wears thin beneath me.
I am standing
     in the dark
          my hands reaching for her photograph;
               the glass so cold
against my face.

              *

The leaves that tremble
          whenever I touch you
               begin to dance;
               branch after branch
heaves inside me.
                  The cats
scrambling each broken wall
                    at last
fear the dogs
                    prancing
around my bitter breath.

It is the breathing
     I cannot forget,
          how rough it is against her
lips;
how my fingers
     could never smooth the broken edges of her sleep.

It
is the breathing I cannot forget.

How
in the middle
of the night

she tears the air with her teeth
how
the air rests
rattling
against the bones inside her,
the bones lose,

or lost.

*

It is morning
my mother is leaving;

I have lain awake all night
watching the thin blue light inside
my room.
I hear the car
start inside the garage.
I rise to slip between my
mother's sheet;

I
smell the blood that has left her lungs the night before.
The sun is
rising between the venetian blinds.

I twirl a cuff of sheet and suck the knot with my teeth.
With my
tongue
I massage the wet knob inside my mouth.
Carefully

                                        the sheet
is drawn back into my
                                throat.
I count.
        I sleep. I am once more inside my mother's arms.
                                The room in
which we lie

splashed with our warmth.
When she turns me to her breast,
                        her soft flesh cracks;
                                Where her breasts
bleed
                                                        I

suck.

                        *

I enter the street.
                I am searching for the right tree to touch.
                                        I run my
palm

against the elm in the parkway.
No answer.

I walk across the lawn
                to the neighbor's liquid amber.

Still no answer.

Slowly I walk down the street,
                my fingers
                                stroking the trunks of
trees.

This morning,
        you are to touch

only the leaves.
spread the meat from their stems
lace the veins across your lips.

Feel your breath inside you.
Tap the lean trees gently,
dig your nails into the bark,
listen to the
green tongues lap at the cold

air,
and where the bark bleeds
lift your tongue to the bitter sap.
Now
put your ear to the trunk;
there is an ache
inside the wood;
tap the
sore

until it is flat and quiet.
Now
listen to your own ache,
tap your heart softly.

Remember,

blood is blood,
fat and thick drying to the bark,
or
thin and brown,
drying to the
neck of a sheet.

Remember,
blood is blood.
Tap
your heart gently—

My right hand rises to my breast,
                          and my fingers
drum agains the heat of my blood,
                     my blood quiets.
                              The voice

inside me grows still
                                   slips into the

dry branches of my lungs;
the thin leaves
                     of my mother's breath lie waiting,

where her weathered hands
take my voice by the throat
                     squeeze its life from inside

me.
I sleep again inside her flesh,
                              trunk inside

trunk,

branch inside branch,
leaves splayed once again to light.

                     *

Come back.
          I turn and walk back to the porch.
                                   Put your

glove on the porch.
I lay the fat leather beside me.
                     Leave two fingers in your

pocket
                                   and tap

three fingers against your thigh.
Too close to your dick. Better.
                     Who is she?
                              Her name is

Connie Murphy.

She's dumb.
I love her.
                    I love my mother.
                        Why did she leave?
She has tuberculosis.
                    That's what your father says.
                                        Where's
your father?
He's at work.
            Your father's a cop and you steal;
                                    Your
father's a cop and you steal
And your mother's inside a sanitarium.
                                Sanitariums are
for the crazy.

My mother has tuberculosis.
Your mother's crazy;
                your mother walks like she's crazy.

Keep tapping your fingers.
Mrs Bains is crazy.
                Mrs Bain's held your hands behind
your back
                                        and her
son beat you with a hose
Mrs Bains is in a sanitarium.
                        Keep tapping.
                            Your dog is
coming down the street, don't
Call it, don't call, don't pet it;
                    or I'll kill your mother inside
the sanitarium.

        Where's your father?
Your father's at work and you steal.
                            Don't pet your dog;
don't let him lick your face.
Keep tapping.
            Connie Murphy is dumb.

                                   Let him lick
your face.

If you cry
I'll make you play with yourself.
                         Keep tapping.

When do you go see your mother?
                              Sunday.
Hold your breath. Count. Keep tapping
                              Your father
kills people.

                         *

On opposite driveways
                    outside houses without trees,
there are two rows of children;
                              each child holds the
hand of he other.

We are no longer children.
There is grass
              in front of our feet to run through;
                                        into the
arms of the other children.
         The dogs on the sidewalk lie without shadow.

A child dashes into the game to break the web.
                                   The sun peels
through the hair of the child falling.
The tongues of the dogs slide onto the cement.
                         Back and forth the children
run into each other's arms.
The runt grass broken sprays from their shoes.
                              The sweat breathes and
bleeds from a dog's nose
And is tongued.

One child dashes after the other;
and their young
arms brace agains the blows.
Far down the block
children too young to play, listen.
Inside
the houses venetian blinds
Slat against the heat;
lips sip lips, an add torn from the
paper.
Inside the children's arms the blood vessels break, bleed,
and still
they stand against the other,
On the other blocks
the lines form to the same hunger,
names
are called;

bodies buck and bend.
the dogs rise towards trees in other yards.
For each bone shocked
another lies waiting.

*

When can I see her?
When's she's no longer contagious.
What does she look like?
Different, better.
Are her cheeks still gone from her face?
Her cheeks are coming back.
Are there stains on her lips from the bleeding?
The bleeding has stopped.
Is her throat all right?
The veins no longer break in her
neck.
Do they comb her hair?
Yes, they comb her hair.

Does she smell?
>She no longer smells.
How are her hands?
>Her strength is returning.
Does she still drop her glass?
>No, she holds onto her glass.
Does she still speak soft?
>Yes, she speaks soft.
Do you kiss her lips?
>I am a voice inside you.
But, are they still inside her face?
>No, her lips are filling out.
Do her eyes roll back?
>Only when it is time for sleep.
Can she hear you speak?
>No, only you.
She's better?
>Yes, she's better.
What was it like when they broke her ribs?
>To remove the lung?
Yes.
>She was asleep.
Sometimes you are loud when I sleep.
>I know, you are angry.
I hope she does not hear you.

*

It is dark.
>Not out there.
In here.
>It is dark.
>Not between the leaves
>>where the bark peels
between my thoughts.
In here
>where the flesh peels between my thoughts.
Not out there

In here
            where the bones of my face
                        rock beneath
my skin;
Where the muscles of my eyes
                        are reaching
                        Yes, not out
there.

                        Not out there,
                        where the light
smacks bright between my eyes.
In here,
            beneath the street,
                        where my thoughts sweep;
                                    back and forth
                                    back and forth.

It is dark
            leaves fall too soon
                        the bark hangs, wet strips from each
branch,
tar dries slowly against the bruised limbs;
                        the teeth of the saw cut
on the upstroke.
Not out there.
Not out there.
In here
where the bones of my face rock.

                        *

Error.

Fingers curled inside the chain link fence
                        catcher's glove between
my thighs.

Error.

The glove
        falls from the brace of my knees;
                        I rock the loose fence
into me.
I count the hops again;
                one, two, three
put the glove down,
                subtract one,
put the glove down
                four, five,
subtract one
                between your legs,
put the glove down.

Error.
        Hold onto the fence;
                        rock.
                        Rock the sun beneath the
trees,

beneath the streets.
Rock the sun in and out,
                in and out.
Rock the sun between your legs;
                        in and out, in and out.
Don't move.
Keep rocking.
Rock the shadows;
in and out,
        in and out.
                Rock the shadows through the doorways;
                                through the falling
leaves.
Rock the shadows between the wires;
                        back and forth
                        back and forth

In and out
        in and out

Rock the shadows through the sun;
                              through your
lips and eyes.
Rock the shadows inside your head.

Count.

                    *

Father,
        I love your silhouette
                as it turns the corner
                              in the warm
September air;
Your hands never in your pockets,
                always loose and free,
                                    the
smoke of a cigarette

climbing your fingers;
your fingers moving to your lips,
                and back again to your heavy stride.

I am standing in the driveway,
                a ball and glove in my hands
                                            as
you take me in your arms,

        into the house.

You pour yourself a drink of bourbon,
                        take the gun from your
holster,

place it on the table.
I don't remember talking,
                watching your face
                        climb the edge of the

glass

until your eyes rested above its lip,
your cheek finding the rim,
                    massaging itself
                              until the tears poured
from your eyes,
and the tears breaking like bits of ice across your lips.
                                                            I

remember counting the tears,
                    sucked back into your mouth;
one,
two,
three,
four,
five,
six,
          and
you surrendered, father;
                    not
like the yellow moth of morning,
                    but
the blue moth of evening,
clinging to the warmth of your glass.

                              *

It is Sunday.
          There are petals in my pocket,
                              petals from the rose I
tried to save you.
It is Sunday.
          The ash of your skin
                    covered with a thin rouge,
                                        the
rouge of morning.
It is Sunday,
          Elysian Park

                    is filling with a brown flesh,
                                    flesh that smells
of roses.
It is Sunday,
        A thousand newspapers
                        spread across the grass,
                                        the grass
smelling of the love of night,
                    the love of flesh inside that night.
It is Sunday.
        There are petals in my pocket,
                        petals from the rose I saved
for you.
It is Sunday.
        The ash of your skin
                        covered with a thin rouge.
It is Sunday.
        There are red apples
                        on the leaves of cactus,
apples whose thorns
            I will kick through the grass for you,
                            thorns I would wear
for you,
Mother of ash,
            Mother of thin rouge.
It is Sunday.
        the leaves are falling
                the sun so far away;
                        I cannot see your face
through the shadows;
the shadows
            taking the light from your eyes,
                                the bell from
your voice.
It is Sunday.
        You wake with half the sanitarium still asleep,
                            with only half
your breath

inside a city still half asleep.

It is Sunday.
     I wake to tap the trunks of angels whose leaves
                               spread
across your ceiling,
your thin fingers,
        slips of green,
                part the blinds;
                        spread
                             as lips
spread
across the amber glass of morning
                  whose lips are basted with
rouge and ash,

whose lips

     seize my lips,
whose breath seizes my breath.

                *

Where the driveway ends
           and the grass begins
                   I am lying in
the dark,
beneath the branches of a lemon tree.

Before the driveway ends,
         as the night begins,
                   soft bare feet
are dancing.
The lights over the pavement are blue
              red, yellow, and white,
                  the lights hung inside
hoops of bright paper.

The lanterns sway above the dancing children;
            with dragons wrapped around

them,
                                                                the
lanterns sway.
Where the driveway ends
                    and the grass begins
                                tables are spread with
red cloths,
green bottles and blue metallic cups,

                                *

The lights
            over the pavement
                                stretch each shadow;
White skirt and black pant flung against the walls.

I do not want to touch the leaf or the bark,
                                and I know to stand
                                        is to rise forever
into the weak stems.
Through the moist stems
                to the final root
                                soft bare feet are dancing.
                                                I
I know to stand
                is to rise forever
                                into the thick fruit.

With Coca-Cola and confetti, dancing.

                                *

The arms that wrap around me
                                are not my own.
Brown fingers stroke my wrists,
                    the face close to mine smelling of

roses.
"Why don't you dance child?
                    Connie saved you some Coca-
Cola.
Come now child, and dance."

I saw her last night while I was sleeping,
she handed me something barely breathing.

There are flowers in her hair,
                    long red petals drawn through black
braids,

I saw her last night inside my dream,
she showed me how to splice,
weave the sack.

In the darkness the pale fruit hangs above us;
                    my face the color of the
lemon,
                    Connie's mother's face the
color of the branch.

I saw her last night;
I could not stop the bleeding.

The earth and the grass grow warm beneath me,
the light broken by branches patches my sin;
for a moment there is only the smell of of flowers
and then the music again slips in.

                         *

It is Monday,
          there is no one to wake me,
The white shade turning yellow in the morning light.
There is no one to wake me,

                    the radio playing in my father's
bedroom;
the red alert in-bound on the San Bernardino Freeway.
It is Monday,
        I am not hungry,
                and I will forget to brush my teeth.
It is Monday,
Freddie will be waiting for me at the first gate,
                        past two poles no bike
could ever fit between.

                    *

You should have told her to dance with him.
        You should have told her,
                One dance,
                    One.
                You should have told her,
                        but no words
came from the dark grass.

You should have told her why.
        One dance
            one
                    would never be
enough.

You should have told her, why.

                    *

It is Monday
        there is no one to wake me,
                each leaf clinging to the
branch.

There is no one to wake me,
            the sidewalks
                        rising to the roots
                                    buckle,
the thin bark shrinks to the trunk.

                    *

Why don't you mention your brother?

He is different from the rest,

How can you tell him apart?

By the spaces between his words.

How long?

Not how long, how short.

Where is he when the games are played?

On his knees between the seats.

Does he have a girl?

Sometimes I hear him leave in the night.

What happens when he returns?

His lips move and he does not sleep.

Where is he when you visit your mother?

He stays to kneel a second time.

And when he returns?

His lips move but he does not eat.

What should I say if we should meet?

You haven't a chance against the voices inside him.

And if he should need me one day?

There are no ends to the voices inside him.

I think I remember him,
always eats alone
even the priest a little afraid?
You haven't a chance against the voices inside.

*

Is Joey really different?
                His words splinter and bleed inside
him.

Mother tells me,

        don't worry.
I told her on Sunday,
                I am afraid.
                She says,
                        he wants to be born
inside the body of Christ.
Can he do that?

He doesn't play anymore;
If Freddy pushes him down,
he lets him spit on him.
                Can he do that?
Father doesn't say, don't worry.
Father went to the priest,
Joey was inside kneeling.
Father screamed at him to get up.
The priest helped my brother,
and asked him to go home.
Can he do that?
Joey Doesn't say a thing,
but his lips are always moving.

*

All of the house are the same.

Everyone builds their own wall.

Take your pills,
drink you juice,
Freddy will wait.
        Where's your brother?

Some walls are higher than the others.
        Take your time.
The houses come in four colors.
        Don't leave,
        one more pill,
        one.
Turquoise, pink, grey, and green.
        Twelve pills to breathe with.
Each house has its own number.
                One pill at a time.
Everyone plants their own lawn.
        Check the stove.
Some are Dichondra.
        Stand up.
The wall inside each house keep the voices down.
        Freddy's waiting.
Even so we are able to hear each other.
        Where's your brother?
The yards are wide enough to play Red Rover.
        Between the seats.
Or steal the bacon.
        Between the seats.
The yards are too short to pitch the distance in.
        Both of you;
            between the seats.
Everyone is white, Jewish, or Italian.

you're eleven years old
and you want to marry Connie Murphy.
Three blocks from here everyone is Mexican.
And your brother wants to marry Christ.
And the houses are all the same.
Between the seats.
And everyone builds their own wall.
Everyday
after school,
Between the seats.

*

In a dark garage,
Freddy plays with his sister's dolls.
He lifts the skirt of one,
he takes the pants off the other.
He asks the girl doll,
Would you like
to dance?

No answer.

Leaves are spread over a doll,
laid in paper and tar;
beneath her head he piles dry twigs.

Barely enough smoke to fill the rafters.

Freddy tells the girl, don't
don't be afraid,
and takes her to dance.

Freddy sits, bruised cheek on a tattered sleeve,
hissing saliva back into his
mouth.
The wire stretched to hold the greased walls of the garage

                                      weaves between
his fingers.
Weaves between his fingers,
                   wire tugging against flesh
                         until the palms flex

in.
The cat in Freddy's lap no longer trembles.

                       *

Four in the morning,
My father does not knock before he enters.
          My father is looking for a gun
               whose barrel is grooved like no
other;
                     a short barreled gun,
                       whose aim
slouches past twenty yards.
My father does not knock before he enters.
              My father's gun is drawn.
                 My father's aim
does not slouch past twenty yards.
There are no women or children inside these rooms
               The floors of these rooms are
less than twenty yards.
The smoke inside each room begins to settle.
             The green walls are yellow,
and the mattresses
                   soaked with
sweat before dawn.
Before dawn,
      soaked in the sour smell of nicotine and sleep.
Before dawn,
      my father is searching;
          my father is searching for the hand
whose aim was true at less than twenty yards.
My father does not knock

before he enters he smells another
smoke,
a sick sweet smoke
          cooking in a spoon for a man he has never
met,
a different kind of a man.
                   A man whose face is the color of
white smoke rising.
My father does not knock before he enters.

          *

A cat screaming like a child;
          no light on in the kitchen.
Where's father?
       A cat screaming.
It is still dark,
       birds wake in the trees.
Is that a child screaming?
       Beaks preen behind leaves,
quickly preen,
       before light.

Before light,
       dusk before dawn,
the sky filling with feathers.
       Is that a child or a cat?
The sky is the color of blood,
       is the color of fire.
I cannot tell.
I cannot tell,
The freeway and the refrigerator start;
               where's father?

Is that a child?

*

The rain inside the parking lot is golden, is light;
                              like dust swept from a
bright room.
My father's face wrinkles, sniffs
                    blanches to the bone.
My father is lifting the body of a man
                    he can smell and feel,
barely see in the darkness.
                    The curtains are heavy with
the crust of smoke,

the grease of hair.
My father opens a window,
                    there is no breeze for the shade to lift
from.
Below, in the parking lot,
                    the rain falling is golden,
                              is light.
Inside the room,
          the feet of the man drip from the bed,
                    blue veins
punched beneath his skin.
One leg of the man's pants rolled above his calf,
                    his flesh knotted and baked by
needles.
In the parking lot below,
                    white bricks are turning the color of
lemons;
my father's face wrinkles, sniffs
                    blanches to the bone.

FIVE STREET

I have been here before,
face twisted on a broken tooth,
eyes poached shut from sleeping in the sun;
then, wandering too close to town
to wake inside this guttered cell;
I have been here before, yes,
curl and shake around my laceless shoes.

*

Started by leaving whenever I could,
easy as calling my name.
Walk all night,
walk all night,
somebody must had a bottle,
always loved it,
warm on my full tongue,
and heat me down,
and heat me down.
Started by:
leaving whenever I could,
always asking people,
"What day is this?
"The Lords Day,"
always say to me;
easy as calling my name.
Easy as calling my name,
the hose turned on inside this tank
to spray me down...
my teeth are bleeding,
my teeth are bleeding,
my tongue flops back,
between my teeth,
are bleeding.

*

Somebody must had a bottle,
always loved it;
before soup and bread,
before mother or father...
Walk all night.
Walk all night.
Doorways close;
beneath the stairs
I lie me down,
clamp the bottle
between my thighs.
To lie here,
crapped and shake,
trying to remember
what it was I left to find.
Or was it just emptiness
I tried to leave behind?
Slipping past my father's urine sheets
and bloody switch at ten, I swear,
it was not his disease I was looking for.
Yet, sometimes, the pain
bleeding sticky white across my lips
falls asleep;
and for a moment I have no hunger.

I have no hunger.
before soup or bread:
no hunger.
Before thy mother
and thy father:
no hunger.
And I lie here,
O Lord,
crapped and shake,
to wait in line

for soup or bread,
always saying to myself,
"Our Father."
And after:
a man takes me by the arm to ask,
"Would you like to go to a meeting brother,
listen to a man
who recovered from your terrible disease?"
I went,
to sit beside a fellow
who scratched and scratched;
to take a can from his coat,
sprays his neck,
his arms,
the soiled folds of his clothing
down...
Until the man next to him
grabbed his arm to say,
"George, easy George,
the bugs you feel
are beneath your skin."

*

Sometimes,
now,
I lie here with my wife to sip,
and remember, finally,
what it was I left to find...
In darkness I watch myself
making love to a woman I once knew,
I did, once, so long ago;
dry for three years,
I loved her as though she could not bleed.
and when she bled,
I left,
simply

of her mortality.
Mortality,
mortality,
pitiful
incomprehensible:
whenever I loved you,
my tongue flopped back;
mortality.

*

The doorway closed above the stairs,

and for a moment,
for a moment,
I saw a shadow beneath me
curl and shake,
and wait:
For money?
For clarity?
I don't know,
but again I knew the hunger
so close to death,
wanting to die,
my only fear not waking:
jacked like a knife,
scraps of myself
scattered around the path of my sleep.
I do not wake, I do not wake,
to see what might be missing.
Do you understand?
Without my wife I have no pulse,
no breath,
no hands to grab my wife,
my flesh would peel between each layer of skin,
until the muscle snaps dry bone,
the ribs in terror crushed by a breath,

a cough, a final laughter.

*

To see what may be missing,
leave the stairs, walk into the street:
No wine.
tongue flaps against my shin,
hands snap at the air,
pants fill with water:
No wine.
A bus crossed Fifth Street for Denver,
if I stumble, if I fall...
NO wine,
no wine,
I loved you as though you could not bleed,
breasts perfect jars from which I sipped,
and bled...
You could not see me,
the dog,
the rat,
whose thin hides
cracked each time
another dark thought screamed inside of me:
No wine.
No wine,
someone takes me by the hand,
no wine,
barefoot,
holding my shoes,
no wine,
wants to take my shoes,
never take my shoes,
curl and shake around my shoes,
no wine...
my feet are bleeding
my feet are bleeding

the skins of my feet flop back;\like fish
are bleeding.
Like claws,
my fingers snap my stiff pants down,
again, and again,
each pair smaller than the last,
until the bare skin
burns against the bones of my ass;
poking through like torn dog,
and rat.

                        *

Now my body leaps inside this room.
The palms of my hands
open and close without permission.
The rags around my wrists
soak,
shrink,
beneath my eyes,
the light is burning,
above
the dark salts the bloody wads
inside my throat:
rise,
clump,
rise,
my tongue slaps their pulse...
Beside me a man smokes,
the dim light between his hands...

                        *

I wake,
and he bleeds my teeth with a spoon;;
presses the gums so the blood runs down the handle:
"The roots are dead,"

says to me,
"all the roots are dead."
The handing me a bottle,
"Have a little for the hands,
you gonna dance again,
soon,
I know, I know,
I danced this ice before,
but I ain't dancin' more for no bottle..."

*

When I dance for the last time,
I am lying across the river,
my father's switch beside me...
I swear,
I danced,
I swear,
it was not his disease I was looking for...
Still the hounds crossed the banks
to lay their tongues upon me...
I swear
the roots were dead,
all the roots were dead,
brittle threads,
whose light steeped muddy terror...
I swear,
they were dead,
dead tongues and hides,
to heat my quaking flesh;
dead,
I swear,

no more for no bottle.

A TRUE STORY
In memory of so many

Let me recite how history repeats itself, history repeats
itself

History, the bus,
                  the bus, history, repeats itself,
            the bus driver,
                    hitler,
                        and my roommate

in the halfway really halfway house,
half way to group therapy,
                today, really,
                      believe me
                                the bus

driver,

hitler,

        on the bus today
repeats itself,
            like father,
                    repeats itself
                          driving the bus

today

        like father,

touched me

      not
my heart not my heart
                and,
my roommate said,
                did you know,
my father
            touched me,

and said,

have I touched you?

and I said,

have you touched me?

and,

my roommate said,

if my father touched me,

and your father touched you

and the bus driver repeats,

like history,

when's when?

*

Let me recite how history repeats itself, history repeats
itself,

the trees

above the trees above me

leaf by leaf the plums,

the plums beneath the leaves, the black birds above,
Oh!
there are so many ways to look at the blackbirds ,

the

plums,
I left today, for you, today, in the ice box,

were they were

they plums?
and,

were the plums inside of plums inside of
blackbirds?

and,

as,

the great sky flashes

                    and
the great sea yearns,
                    and as,
                              we ourselves flash and yearn,

and,

  as my mother told me, repeatedly, you have no inner
resources,

I now admit
I have no inner resources,
                    and,

                              though,
the great sky flashes and the great sea yearns,
                                        and as,
we ourselves flash and yearn,

for mother?
          for father?
for someone in the group to believe me that hitler touched
me

today

        touched me,
yesterday,
          today,

I must ask,
            but,
                  do i ask,
      if there are only thirteen ways of looking at a
blackbird
                                        and if
the plums in the ice box
were so delicious, is hitler driving a bus as dangerous as it
seems?

yes.

*

Let me recite how history repeats itself, history repeats.

As dangerous as it seems
                              in the half way halfway house
mrs mrs is nice

                    but
sometimes she is from hitler,
                              when is she from hitler?
                                                        When
        i do not do not want to take my medication
                                        because i know

the food is poisoned so poisoned
like history poisoned,
                    like father,
                                repeats itself.

History
        poison,
                my brother,
                                poison,
        came to visit me yesterday,
                                and,
                                        poison says,

i am sick

                and,
                        take your medication
        or,
                they will put you back in restraints!
                                                I
told him
the problem that is the the problem is not my medication

the problem

                    is
hitler driving the bus
                              now
                        i
asked him did daddy do, daddy do, like a big black shoe?

not your heart, not your heart?
and he said that
                        that was a long time ago
                                          and
he doesn't
              dig up
                              so i
told him
        history repeats itself brother
                              let me recite how
history repeats and he said
                              the past is the past

and
he only wants me to start

                              over
                                    because
mrs mrs is nice and doesn't want me back in restraints, i,
                                                      i
heard

him say it,
he said, start
              and
                  i said brother i want to start, start all
over again,

but,

        brother, I can't
because I have no inner resources and hitler is driving the
bus.

PART 3: SPRING STREET

I

It all seemed to happen without you, spinning like a bottle
on the floor of your daughter's dorm room, all the boys
sitting, terrified to kiss the wrong girl.

At night, sounds in the kitchen soothe you. As does traffic.
Without her head in the crook of your arm you pull the
sheet tight. Shadows on the ceiling weave together as your
arms and legs, once entwined with hers, twitch, dance like
someone who has had too much to drink, and you have.
Like all animals you sing. Each note in your sleep turning
your head towards the songs you learned to sing after
your parents began shutting the door to their room. You
listened. You sang. You could not stop washing your
hands. When your father left, you watched your mother
smoking in the kitchen, staring at the floor, rising to walk
to her car, backing out her car.

Eventually, you learned water could speak. During the
stings of insects and the cold showers each night, water
spoke to you, and you told no one. Not because you were
afraid of what people would think, but because of what the
water told you. About time and about the color green, how
someday, without water, time will stop trying to wake you
each morning, and without anything green to hold on to,
time will stop trying to wake us all.

It all seemed to happen without you, a bottle spinning on
the floor of your room, all the boys sitting, terrified to kiss
the wrong girl.
Streets, not far from here line up with tents. As a soldier
of a different war, inured to the bodies vanishing over
nights whose screams waft from tent to tent, the dreams of
rape continue like waves whose shores sink beneath your
feet, the soft sleep of heroin washed down with wine closes
your eyes and you no longer wake up screaming inside
dreams of a boy taking off your pants and you waking up as
he enters you.
In the shops inside the diamond district you can ask for a
tea or a coffee and they know you are not buying because
you smell like everyone smells five blocks from here,
cigarettes, wine, and nylon, and they are nice to you and
wonder, what happened to this white girl.
Between the freeways, downtown waits for the lawyers to
arrive each morning, their suits wrinkled, many trying to
remember last night. Your attorney smells of bourbon,
you ask him if he needs some speed. He looks at you like
an insect slipping on wet glass, you look back like someone
whose last dream was weeks ago because the drugs are
working.
It was at night. Both of your parents were working late,
preparing a case for the next day, taking a client out for
dinner. Everyone came at the same time. Everyone put
their pills onto the wood floor. With the first bottle of Jack
Daniels empty, someone began spinning it and the first
couple kissed. Usually the sun sets on time. You can set
your watch to it. You can set your watch to the sun rising
also. People who live in tents eventually sell their watch if
they have one. The color of

the day and it's shadows tell the time and the day is simply
a knot tied ahead of the last knot. The most important
possession is your tent, your bed, and the zipper to your
tent. That no one knows if you are inside or not is like
having money in the bank, or love and trust, parents who
are there for dinner each night.

At night, sounds in the kitchen soothe you. As does traffic. Without her head in the crook of your arm you pull the sheet tight. Shadows on the ceiling weave together as your arms and legs, once entwined with hers, twitch, dance like someone who has had too much to drink, and you have. You are looking for a house, a house close to water, close to a long shore to walk at night because you are now in love with silence, the kind of silence leaves grow in slowly, leaves that rustle in the wind, like a bride putting on her new dress over her head.

Your daughter taught you love and hate, you hold them up to a matter of perception. So you talked to no one and no one talked to you about her absence.

To get to her, you have to go through Tip Toe. Tip Toe knows her tent. Tip Toe Knows everyone. Tip Toe can fix you up.

The books all over the tent surprise you. The class schedule taped to the tent pole amazes you.

The problem has always been water. Whether it's finding a way to live next to it, or just finding it. You have never told anyone that water speaks to you. You never will. No one will ever learn about your rituals in the bathroom. The only time you worried, your wife mentioned the high cost of a water bill. You were also amazed by the pictures taped on the ceiling of the tent. Pictures of villages in Scotland. Pictures of cows in pastures. Pictures of vines hanging from trees. She had written herself a note, "if water talks to you don't listen, make sure you stay awake, only listen to ice, before it becomes water, when the ice is still a cliff high above the sea, before the sun burns wholes in it, before anyone starts to drown.

Like all animals you sing. Each note in your sleep turning
your head towards the songs you learned to sing after your
parents began shutting the door to their room. You listened.
You sang. You could not stop washing your hands. When
your father left, you watched your mother smoking in the
kitchen, starring at the floor, rising to walk to her car,
backing out her car.

You are trying to take off the legs of an ant. You and your
friends cover the ants you have collected in spit. You are lying
on your bare backs on the hot cement. The guy from Water
and Power is tightening the bolt of the hydrant. You look up
at the sky. A kid from a different block joins you, asks if you
want to buy a bike. When the police arrive. You tell them you
haven't seen anyone but the guy from Water and Power.
When the police leave your friends start laughing. They ask
you why you are crying. Somebody passes around a pack of
cigarettes.

You walk past your house. You walk a long time. You take
off your shoes. You cool your feet with a hose. You put your
shoes back on. The stores are still open. You walk into a
seven eleven. You look at stuff. You walk out. The kid behind
the counter follows you. You run to the dump nearby. You
are poking at trash with a broken broom when the car drives
up. Gulls fly over the mounds of trash. In spring through
summer poppies bloom. You pick the poppies for your
mother on Mother's Day. You hand over the candy bar.
When they put you in the back seat they tell you they are only
going to take you home. When you start to sing, you are told
not to. The songs in your head never stop.

5

Eventually you learned water could speak. In between the stings of
insects and the cold stems you climbed at night, water spoke to you,
and you told no one. Not because you were afraid of what people
would think, but because of what water had told you. About time and
about the color of green. How, someday, without water, time will
stop trying to wake you each morning, and without anything green to
hold onto, time will stop trying to wake us all.

To plow is to know the earth and to know the earth is to know the
swarms of insects that stay close to light, unknown in the dark, spied
upon by those who live upside down in caves or cliffs hanging above
a sea you walk all day to find, to be completely alone, to think quietly
about the fate of boats pulled by hand to land.

You want to join them, live in the same small villages. Where the
cows enter each day on their way to higher pastures, and where each
night you sit with friends holding each other straight, knowing that
as long as there is sea there is still time for someone's dreams to
catch a skiff and disappear.

Of course, a moth at the window knows no one, and this is how you
feel. So you walk back. That you were not missed was no surprise as
no one believed you could leave. Which is sad, but it is sad to feel no
sadness at all. It could be worse.

There could be no vines hanging over the walls, so no escape. Some
nights it looks as if you are going to have to ring the bell everyone
knows to leave by. But in the morning, when the stems are still green
and there is water dripping from each roof, you slow down, breathe
deeply, wait to see if the others still agree.

POSTSCRIPT: THE NIGHT OF THE LIVING BUKOWSKI

Charles Bukowski read at the University of Santa Cruz in 1972. It was a big event, Bukowski, following Harold Norse's inclusion of his work in the Penguin Anthology of Contemporary American Poets (1969), was now a mainstream American poet reading in the U.S. and Europe. It was a big event for several reasons, one of them being that the continent had apparently shifted and many important American writers were now gathering in Santa Cruz: Ray Carver, George Hitchcock, William Everson (formerly Brother Antoninus), Peter Beagle, Ron and Lynn Sukinek, Mary Korte, Morton Marcus, and Joe Stroud, to name a few. Gerard Malanga, Andy Warhol's photographer, had arrived to document in film the literary phenomena occurring in Santa Cruz, and magazines and newspapers like The Bay Area Guardian were documenting the Santa Cruz literary scene.

Santa Cruz was going through a literary renaissance. Ray Carver had moved to Santa Cruz and would start the magazine, Quarry West, and George Hitchcock was publishing American Surrealist poetry out of his magazine Kayak. The young poets mentored by Morton Marcus, Joe Stroud and George Hitchcock were phenomenal, both in numbers and in talent. A group of young poets, Paul Mann, Stephen Kessler, Bill Greenwood, and Tom Maderos formed Green Horse Press, publishing their own work as well as Spanish and French poetry in translation. Gary Young, now a renown prose poet eventually established Greenhouse Review Press. Though Morton Marcus, William Everson, and George Hitchcock are no longer with us, Joe Stroud, Stephen Kessler and Gary Young remain in Santa Cruz.

I came to Santa Cruz to write poetry at around 19. I was working as a day laborer in agriculture or in rest-homes. I was not an academic. My literary studies were private. When I was seventeen in Los I started reading European poetry, Rimbaud, Flaubert. But it was the Spanish and Latin American poets that I could not read enough of. Lorca and Vallejo, for example. I did read some contemporary American and British poets: Merwin, Plath, Hughes-- and I noticed at the beginning of each book there was a "thanks to" and I asked someone at the front desk of a bookstore, what the "thanks to" meant. I was told that the thank you was to various magazines. When The Nation published me; when a poem of mine fell out of a short story by Lew Matthews, and they contacted Lew, wanting to know from which language I was translated, and when I wrote back that I was American, they published a poem. It was at this point that I began to try and meet imminent literary figures including Ray Carver, George Hitchcock, Mary Korte, Morton Marcus, Joe Stroud, Peter Beagle, Victor Perera, James B Hall, and my mentor/muse, William Everson. It was then that George Hitchcock presented me in San Francisco and Rolling Stone Magazine included me in their article on the 100 Best Poets In America. This all happened in two years. This two-year period culminated on The Night Of The Living Bukowski.

Bukowski's arrival meant a party which meant a lot of drinking and competition for being noticed. By the time Bukowski arrived, the kinship amongst young writers was sadly devolving into factions and rivalries: Those young poets attending University Of California Santa Cruz, aligned with George Hitchcock and the young poets who lived in town aligned with Morton Marcus. Also, Jim Delesandro, a writer and entrepreneur arrived on the scene, and soon thereafter, rented the largest auditorium in Santa Cruz for a poetry reading. Who was and who was not asked to read further eroded the camaraderie forming since 1970, and all who were asked to read and all who were not asked to read, were all at the party for Charles Bukowski.

As was Ray Carver. Ray Carver was now Ray Carver. The writer who reimagined and reinvented the American short story. Ray Carver and Charles Bukowski had a lot in common and a lot not in common. They were both working class, both struggled to emerge as important American author. However, Ray was part of the "Academy"—attending and teaching at the Master of Fine Arts Programs emerging throughout the United States, and Bukowski loathed the MFA programs and the many perfect poems and stories emerging from these programs. While Ray Carver reinvented the American short story, Charles Bukowski brought to life poems written in everyday language with everyday violence and everyday sex, with the imagination of a Wallace Stevens.

The party, in many ways was uneventful. Both Carver and Bukowski were in the hey day of their drinking, and young poets, like myself, who could drink long into the night, were entering into their own version of self destruction. The highlight of the evening was Charles Bukowski unzipping his pants and flicking his dick at me with a disgusted look on his face because, evidently, I was talking with the young woman he was interested in too long, holding her attention too long. When I cranked my middle finger into the air, back at Bukowski, Bukowski got up and asked me to "take it outside". We climbed down the stairs towards a cement driveway. I remember thinking, Christ, his face really does look like it has been run over by a truck. When we squared off, I asked Bukowski, Charles, are you sure you wouldn't rather have a drink together. Bukowski burst out laughing. We went back up stairs arm in arm and spent a fresh bottle.

What really matters, after forty-seven years, is the promise and the failure of a project that looked like literary heaven only two years before. Before the rifts and the competition, before the slights and insults, Santa Cruz was bursting at the seams with young writers with ample literary figures to look up to and to be guided by. In a way, Bukowski and Carver symbolized what eventually happened to the literary scene in Santa Cruz between 1970 and 1974. Hope and dread, two of their work's major themes. The hope was represented by the fact that for this brief time in history, anyone with a true desire to write could be included into a group with literary figures, now only accessible if you attend an MFA program. The dread is represented by the struggle every writer has to keep their hand in the game. To say that the party with Bukowski and Carver was uneventful is my bias. That it was uneventful is also misleading. Because, almost everyone in that room alive today is, to my knowledge, still involved in the arts. It is misleading because, though the literary commune, so to speak, failed, Santa Cruz went on to become the home of poets like Lucille Clifton, Adrienne Rich, Al Young, Stephen Kessler, Gary Young, and Ellen Bass.

Robert Lundquist
DTLA February 2018

A GATHERING OF SANTA CRUZ AREA WRITERS AT COOPER HOUSE, JUNE, 1973
WINDOW, L. TO R: Morton Marcus, Peter S. Beagle, Anne Steinhardt, Robert
Lundquist, James B. Hall, Stephen Levine, Victor Perera, T. Mike Walker.
STANDING, L. TO R: James D Houston, William Everson, Mason Smith,
SEATED, L. TO R: John Deck, Lou Mathews, Nels Hanson, George Hitchcock

ROBERT LUNDQUIST, 2017

Robert Lundquist is a poet and practicing psychoanalyst in Los Angeles. His poems have appeared in such magazines as The Nation, The Paris Review, Poetry Now, Kayak, Quarry West. Robert was also one of five writers who taught poetry in the prison system in California, afterwards editing an anthology of prose and poetry by the writers in prison entitled About Time II. When Robert is not with his wife, Nazare Magaz, or writing, he is seeing patients in his office above The Last Bookstore in Downtown Los Angeles. Included in his adventures in DTLA was entering Zen Center Los Angeles for two years when he was eighteen and in his adolescence taking harmonica lessons from George Smith in Watts. Robert began to write poetry at twenty and at twenty-one moved to Santa Cruz California to be a part of a literary renaissance in Santa Cruz where he was featured in the magazine Quarry West started by Ray Carver. This is his first full length book.

NEW RIVER
PRESS

FITZROVIA
LONDON